Mel Bay Presents Frequently Aske

CW00819304

FAQ

ELECTRIC GUITAR CARE AND SETUP
By John LeVan

1 2 3 4 5 6 7 8 9 0

Visit us on the Web at www.melbay.com — E-mail us at email@melbay.com

Foreword

Some years back, while walking through my factory, I was introduced to a young man by my then service manager at Taylor Guitars, Terry Myers. "Bob," he said, "this is John LeVan, the guy I've told you about who's got a repair shop going up in Auburn." "Auburn?" I thought, "What kind of business can a guy do in repairs up in Auburn?"

Auburn is a little wooded town just north of Sacramento, California, and among my favorite spots, actually. The year was 1994 and John was determined to become one of our very first authorized service centers. Terry has since moved to other duties at Taylor Guitars, but at the time he was envisioning repairmen across the country that had the talent to work on our guitars the way we would; fast, efficient, and above all, able to diagnose the true problem with the guitar. Terry worked hard on that goal, but he needed raw talent and a good attitude from the applicants in order to accomplish the task.

So here was John LeVan, spending his time in our repair shop learning our guitars, our methods, our diagnosing procedures; he was learning to have our eyes.

Well, he went home to Auburn, and it came to pass that he grew tremendously in knowledge and eventually relocated to Nashville. This was music to our ears because we now had a man in place in Music City, USA to take care of the many, many Taylor owners there. Nashville is the place with probably the highest population of professionals who use our guitars. John established himself there as an expert guitar repairman who could give great service to people who needed it, both the players and us at Taylor. Our relationship with John has been a joy.

We all know the idea of any category being divided into good, better, and best. I see a lot of people who want to do guitar repairs and be an expert at it. But I don't see people who are hungry for knowledge and experience on how to really be an expert, and are willing to put in the time necessary and check their ego at the door in order to learn. This expertise I'm referring to starts with the skill of looking at a guitar and deciding what the problem is. (You have no idea how many times a neck is re-fretted when what the guitar actually needs is to be humidified!) After that, it moves on to the expertise of how to effectively accomplish the repair, all in the given time allotted, and then returning that guitar to its owner at the promised time.

John LeVan has done more than gather knowledge, he has amassed it. When I read this book I see John's habits on the page - look at the guitar, assess the problem, clean the workbench and gather the right tools, wash your hands, put on a smile, and get it done properly, with the least effort.

It's amazing that after less than a lifetime of guitar repair John can be so organized and energized to put it all in the form of a book like this, thus, passing on the information to others. Please take a good look and learn some things from a person who is an expert learner himself.

Bob Taylor

Dedication

I dedicate this book to my wife Wendy and my two daughters, Sarah and Sophia, who every day remind me that life is precious, fragile and miraculous.

Acknowledgments

I would like to thank all of the people who have encouraged, supported and apprenticed me in the craft of luthrie. Special thanks to my Lord Jesus Christ for creating me and giving me a wife that will tolerate me. To my wife, Wendy, for putting up with me for all of these years. Lt. Col. John Nargiso Bilson, for making a man out of me. Brad Shreve, the first person to teach me anything about guitar repair. Karl (with a 'K') Mischler, for teaching me how to play the guitar. Michael Lewis, for including me in the creation of the Sacramento Valley Luthiers Guild. Bob Taylor and Terry Myers, for believing in me enough to let me study at the Taylor® Guitar Factory and showing me how a real repair shop is run, and for the great photographs and diagrams. Tom Anderson®, for affording me the opportunity to learn an excellent technique of fretwork, and opening my eyes to a new temperament. Everyone at Gruhn® Guitars, for all of their support and friendship, especially Ben Burgett and Andy Jellison for teaching me the most cutting-edge repair techniques. Seymour Duncan®, thanks for all the great diagrams, support and products. Lloyd Baggs from L.R. Baggs®, the excellent pictures, product and information for the book. Jay Hostetler from Stewart-MacDonald® for providing us with great tools. Skip Anderson, for invaluable advice. Finally, all of the good people who have trusted me with their instruments. Without all of you, I'd probably still be working in a gas station.

Chapter 8: Top 10 Signs of a Problematic Guitar 59

Chapter 9: Other Upgrades and Repairs 63

Chapter 10: Other Training Resources 74

Guitar Repair and Maintenance Kit

It's important to use the correct tool for the job. Likewise it is important to buy quality tools that will last. The quality of your tools is reflected in your work, and your work is your calling card. Every guitar you work on is like a résumé, so be sure to do your best. Below is a list of tools and materials recommended to perform the tasks outlined in this book. Here is what you need to get started:

6-Piece Screwdriver Set	**Straight Edge**
6-Piece Miniature Needle File Set	**Vacuum (with brush attachment)**
Precision Scale (rule)	**Toothbrush**
14-Piece Hex Key Set	**Nut Drivers**
10-Piece Nut File Set	**X-Acto® Knives**
String Winder	**Magnifying Lamp**
Cordless Drill	**Guitar Tuner**
Wire Cutters	**Humidifier**
Polish Cloth	**Safety Glasses**

The six-piece screwdriver set should include a small, medium and large-tip Phillips-head screwdriver, and a small, medium and large-tip flathead screwdriver. These will be used for adjustments such as intonation, neck bolts, pickgaurd screws, pickups, etc.

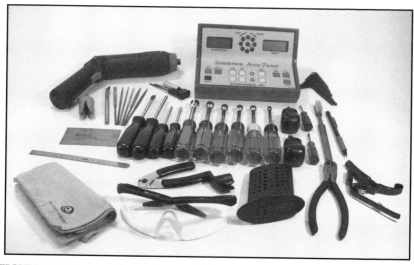

FIGURE 1.1 Here are the tools you will need to complete the projects in this book. (Photo by John LeVan)

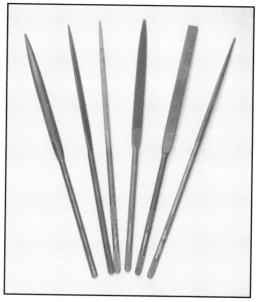

FIGURE 1.2 The six-piece miniature needle file set should be single-cut, Swiss, and made of carbide steel. (Photo by John LeVan)

Your file set should include:

1. Round File
2. Flat File
3. Square File
4. Half-Round File
5. Three-Cornered File
6. Flat Triangular File

These files will be used to carve and intonate a bridge saddle, file fret ends, spot level a fret, clean out a slot in a string nut, cut slots into a string nut, file the bridge pin holes, etc.

FIGURE 1.3A The precision scale rule is a small, six-inch, metal ruler that measures from 1/64" on up. This is important because many of the measurements in this book are in 1/64" and 1/32". Be sure that your scale has good contrast to make it easy to read. (Photo by John LeVan)

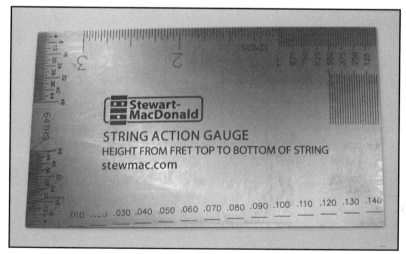

1.3B An Action Gauge® (sold by Stewart MacDonald®) is an excellent tool for measuring the action on a guitar. (Photo by John LeVan)

An important set for your tool collection is a 14 piece hex key set. This set will be used for adjusting bridge saddles, trussrods, some pickup pole pieces, access panels, etc. I recommend the following sizes; .05", 1/16", 3/32", 1/8", 5/32", 9/64", 3/16", 1mm, 1.5mm, 2mm, 2.5mm, 3mm, 4mm, 5mm.

FIGURE 1.4 The 10-piece nut file set is critical to carving a string nut as well as the final steps to a setup. You'll need these sizes; .010, .012, .016, .022, .026, .032, .036, .040, .046, .052. The above listed files are two-sided, made of carbide steel and are absolutely necessary. (Photo by John LeVan)

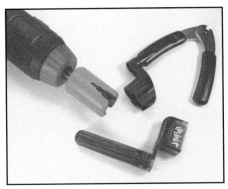

FIGURE 1.5 There are many types of string winders on the market. Varying from $.99 to $29, this is one tool that will save you a lot of time and energy. I prefer the type that sets into a cordless drill, thus speeding up the restringing process and minimizing fatigue and the risk of developing tendonitis. (Photo by John LeVan)

When choosing a cordless drill, I recommend a rechargeable model with a pistol grip, torque clutch, reversible, and at least 500 rpm. As for wire cutters, a six-inch pair of angled pliers works well. The only polish cloth I use in my shop is a 100% cotton, birdseye weave cloth diaper.

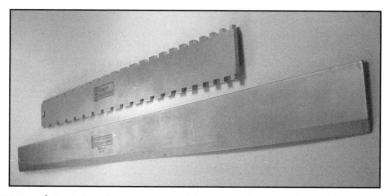

FIGURE 1.6 Straight edges are essential for sighting a neck and checking the frets to see if they are level. There are several sizes and types that I recommend starting from 1", 4", 6", 12", 24" to 36" and even one that is notched out where the frets are to check that the fretboard is true (straight with the proper radius). (Photo by John LeVan)

FIGURE 1.7 A vacuum with a round brush attachment will help you clean up metal filings and dust when working on a guitar. I prefer a small Shop Vac®; however most uprights have all the attachments you need – *just don't tell your spouse I said to use it.* **(Photo by John LeVan)**

A medium to hard bristle toothbrush is perfect for scrubbing while applying lemon oil to your fretboard. *Remember – it's not nice to use someone else's toothbrush without asking first!*

There are nine nut driver sizes that will be the most useful. 1/4", 5/16", 9/32", 11/32", 7/16", 1/2", 9/16", 6mm, 10mm are used for everything from adjusting a truss-rod to tightening an endpin jack. X-Acto® knife sets are very handy around the shop. They come with several types of replacement blades and handles. These are used for scoring, cleaning glue out of a fret slot, etc. Magnifying lamps help you see detail that you normally can't see with the naked eye. Warning – this can be a very humbling experience. An electric drill and bits are needed when boring out the end block to install an endpin jack, installing an acoustic guitar pickup and all those other projects that require more torque than what your cordless drill has. Bits that are needed will be all standard (not metric) sizes from 1/16" to 1/8". You may also want a tapered ream for boring to install an endpin jack.

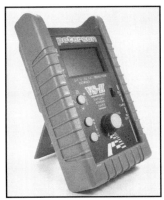 

FIGURE 1.8 There are so many choices when it comes to choosing a guitar tuner. Most tuners are really not accurate enough to intonate a guitar properly. Our shop tuner is accurate to +\- 1/100 of one cent. One note = 100 cent. Most tuners are +/- three to five cent. I recommend a tuner that is at least +/- one cent for intonating a guitar. Most guitar tuners publish their accuracy ratings in their brochures. (Photo by John LeVan)

FIGURE 1.9 Humidifiers are one of the least expensive ways to prevent damage to a guitar. Our shop has warm mist room humidifiers as well as ones you install inside your guitar for transporting and storage. This will be covered in detail in Chapter 2. (Photo by John LeVan)

Always wear your safety glasses. Safety first, convenience second!

Materials:

Here is a list of the most common materials that will be needed for general guitar repair and maintenance.

- Wood Glue (Titebond® I and Titebond® II, RBC® Epoxy)
- Super Glue®, Thick and Thin (Jet® or Zap® brand)
- 1500 Grit Self-Adhesive Sandpaper
- 220 Grit Self-Adhesive Sandpaper
- Super Glue® Accelerator
- Super Glue® Solvent
- 0000 Steel Wool
- Masking Tape
- Guitar Polish
- Suction Cup
- Lemon Oil
- Q-Tips®

FIGURE 1.10 Here are the materials and supplies needed to complete the repairs in this book. (Photo by John LeVan)

Wood glue is needed for structural repairs. Titebond® I is great for neck resets and bridge plate repairs. Titebond® II is better for broken headstocks, body cracks and bridge re-glues. RBC® Epoxy is good for crack repairs that require color matching. It can be mixed with fresco powder to match the paint or lacquer color of the guitar you are repairing. Super Glue® (cyanoacrylite) is manufactured by several companies. Zap® and Jet® are two that have given me great results. They come in a wide range of viscosities, from water thin to the thickness of molasses. We use the ultra thin, thin and thick the most. This type of glue works great for securing a string nut, loose frets and minor touch ups on acrylic and polyurethane finishes. Be sure to also have Super Glue® accelerator (to speed up drying time) and Super Glue® solvent (in case you glue your finger to your chin). Self-adhesive sandpaper is always a must for any repair shop. 1500 grit is best for polishing (burnishing) bone string nuts and saddles. It also comes in handy to sand out finish scratches. 220-grit sandpaper is best for carving string nuts and bridge saddles. When choosing an electronics cleaner, chose one that is safe for all plastics. Some types of cleaner can damage the plastic parts in switches and potentiometers. 0000 Steel wool is needed to do a final polish on the frets as well as clean the fretboard. Never use anything more coarse on a guitar, it could damage the frets. Compressed air is used to remove dust from electronic components. Low-tack 3" masking tape will be useful to tape off pickups while cleaning. Most guitar polishes will work fine on most finishes, just don't use any polish on satin finishes, it will make them look inconsistent and hazy. A small suction cup is excellent for removing those stubborn control panels. Lemon oil is the best substance to condition a rosewood or ebony fretboard. It is highly recommended to con-

14

dition and clean your guitar. Q-Tips® are an absolute necessity whenever you use glue of any type. They are also handy for cleaning those hard to reach places like under a bridge saddle or between your toes. There are several brands available and most are adequate.

Sources:

- LeVan's Guitar Services (615) 251-8884   www.guitarservices.com

- Luthier's Mercantile® (800) 477-4437   www.lmii.com

- Stewart-MacDonald® (800) 848-2273   www.stewmac.com

- All Parts® (800) 327-8942   www.allparts.com

Hygiene

The key to preventing corrosion, cracking and poor guitar hygiene is to clean and condition your guitar every time you change your strings.

One of the most overlooked parts of owning a guitar is cleaning and conditioning it regularly. Why is this so important? Because the more you play your guitar the more dirt, sweat and oils build up on your guitar. As a result, your strings, frets and bridge receive the brunt of the damage. The acid in sweat and the oils from your fingers corrodes the strings causing them to lose their bright tone. Likewise sweat and oils condense on the frets causing the wood around them to deteriorate. If left unconditioned, the fretboard and bridge can and will crack.

So how do you prevent these filthy afflictions from ravaging your guitar? It all starts with good hygiene.

The first step to good guitar hygiene is player cleanliness

- Wash your hands before you play

- Wipe your strings with a clean dry cloth after playing

- Make your *friends* wash their hands before you let them play *your* guitar

- Good hygiene is good guitar care!

It also helps to store your guitar in its case, and occasionally vacuum the case.

Materials Needed:

- 0000 Steel Wool (only 0000, never anything coarser)

- Vacuum (with brush attachment)

- Toothbrush

- Paper Towels

- Masking Tape (only for maple or blond fret board, and/or to cover the pickups on an electric guitar)

- Lemon Oil

- Guitar Polish

Cleaning

There are a few fundamental steps to cleaning your guitar. The first step is to remove the strings - *YES ALL OF THEM*. It does not damage the guitar to remove all strings at one time. Next, you need to scrub the fretboard with 0000 steel wool in the direction of the grain of the wood. This will clean the dirt and grime off of your fretboard as well as polish the frets. **DO NOT USE 0, 00 or 000 steel wool,** *only 0000.* If your guitar has a maple or blonde fretboard, then you'll need to either cover the wood with masking tape (only exposing the metal frets) or skip using the steel wool. 0000 Steel wool is a fine grit steel wool that won't damage the frets or fretboard. Avoid getting it into the electronics or on the finish.

If you are cleaning an electric guitar, be sure to cover the pickups with masking tape to prevent the steel wool from attaching to the pickup coils. The pickup coils are magnetic and will attract the steel wool. A low-tack, 3" or 4" masking tape is recommended for taping off the pickups. Cover them completely to prevent the steel wool from collecting around the pickup. Steel wool can cause the pickup to become microphonic and feedback.

Scrubbing the Fretboard

Scrubbing the fretboard will remove dirt, dead skin cells and other things that collect on your fretboard. You should do this every time you change your strings. The steps are as follows:

- Scrub the frets using the 0000 steel wool "with the grain" of the wood. 99.99 percent of the time "with the grain" is the length of the neck.

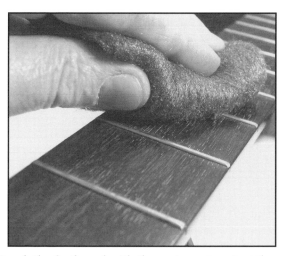

FIGURE 2.1 Scrub the fretboard with the grain, not against the grain. (Photo by John LeVan)

- After the fretboard is clean and the frets are polished, use a vacuum to remove all of the steel wool from the guitar. Make sure you vacuum the entire guitar and around the bench too. Remove masking tape.

Conditioning

Conditioning your guitar is easy. All you need is a toothbrush, lemon oil and paper towels.

- Just dip your toothbrush into the lemon oil and then scrub the fretboard. Make sure that you cover all of the fretboard. A great thing about lemon oil is that you can't over oil your fretboard, it will only absorb what it needs.

- After the lemon oil settles into the wood for a few minutes, simply wipe off the excess with a dry paper towel.

FIGURE 2.2 Most toothbrushes won't damage the fretboard. Don't be afraid of scrubbing it into the wood. (Photo by John LeVan)

Now is a good time to clean the rest of the body using a damp paper towel and a few drops of lemon oil. This process will make your guitar look and perform at its best.

Restringing

After thoroughly cleaning and conditioning your guitar, you are ready to restring. Depending upon what kind of guitar you have (classical, electric, acoustic, bass, etc) there are several techniques that can be applied. For a classical or nylon string guitar, the strings are tied on using a looping method. For an acoustic or bass, there is a standard method to restring. For an electric, it can be complex or very simple depending upon the type of hardware it has.

Tools Needed:

- String Winder (manual or electric)
- String Cutters (end cutters, dykes, nippers)
- Guitar Tuner
- Patience

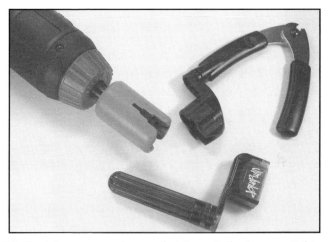

FIGURE 2.3 Electric or manual, a good string winder is essential to restringing a guitar. Likewise, a 6" pair of end cutters and an accurate guitar tuner are a must. (Photo by John LeVan)

Electric guitars can be quite an adventure to restring.

Most electric guitars like the Strat®, Tele® and Les Paul® style guitars, are pretty basic. You just run the string thru either the tailpiece or thru the bridge and then tie the strings onto the tuning key post. Some electric guitars have a locking tremolo system. Locking tremolo systems require hex keys to lock and unlock the string in order to do a restring. Like the acoustic guitar, you only want between three and four wraps around the post. Too few wraps will result in the string slipping out of tune, too many will result in the string stretching out of tune. There are a few techniques that may helpful to you in order to get a uniform wrap for each string.

FIGURE 2.4 A tailpiece holds the strings in place as they lay over the bridge. (Photo by John LeVan)

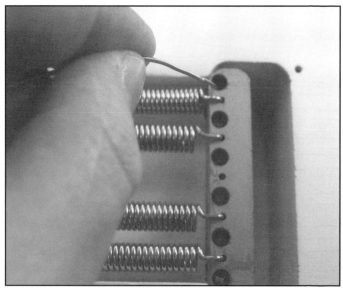

FIGURE 2.5 Tremolo style bridges are strung from behind thru the inertia or tail-block. (Photo by John LeVan)

FIGURE 2.6A,B Locking tremolos require hex keys to lock and unlock the strings from the bridge saddles and at the locking string nut. (Photo by John LeVan)

The bridge assembly includes

- Intonation Screws
- Saddle Height Adjustment Screws
- Inertia Block
- Bridge Saddle
- Bridge Plate
- Tremolo Arm
- Spring Claw
- Tremolo Springs

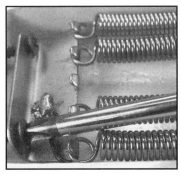

FIGURE 2.7A,B,C The intonation screws are for adjusting (you guessed it) intonation. The saddle height adjustment screws adjust the saddles up and down. The inertia block holds the ball end of the strings and acts as a counterbalance in tandem with the tremolo springs. The spring claw is used to adjust the tremolo flush to the body of the guitar. The bridge plate connects all the other components together. (Photo by John LeVan)

Measure using the posts

To achieve the correct number of wraps, on a guitar with all six keys on one side of the neck, just pull the string three or four posts past the one to which you are going to wrap the string. Then mark the string by bending it where it meets that third or fourth post, this will show you where the string should end when you pull it thru the intended post. For example, when installing the low E string, pull it to the D or G-string post, bend it where it lines up with that post. Then run it thru the low E post up to the bend in the string and begin to wind the string onto the post. Always wind the string downward, never upward or over itself. Wrapping the string over itself can cause string breakage and tuning problems. Finally, tune the guitar using an accurate guitar tuner (see Figure 1.28).

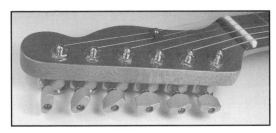

FIGURE 2.8 This guitar has all six tuning keys on one side. This is also referred to as six-in-line. (Photo by John LeVan)

FIGURE 2.9 Bend the string after pulling it three or four posts beyond the one to which you want to tie it. This is an easy and accurate way to mark the end of the string before you start winding it onto the tuning key post. (Photo by John LeVan)

FIGURE 2.10 Always wind the string downward, never upward or over itself. The goal is three to four tight wraps around the tuning key post. (Photo by John LeVan)

Transporting and Storage

When transporting and storing your guitar it's important to do so in a consistent environment. **When shipping a guitar,**

- Slightly de-tune the strings just in case it is jarred while in transit. A sudden impact can cause structural damage when the guitar is under tension.

- Install a fretguard to prevent the strings from damaging the frets if the guitar is dropped or jarred. A piece of cardboard or file folder will work.

- Secure your guitar in a quality ATA-certified guitar case and be sure that it doesn't have any wiggle room. A snug case makes for a safer guitar.

- Place all peripheral equipment in either the storage compartment of the case or in a separate bag. Do not leave anything in the case that can slide, fall or bounce on or into your guitar.

Detuning the strings (a few turns on each key) will help prevent extra tension on the guitar. This is especially important for acoustic guitars.

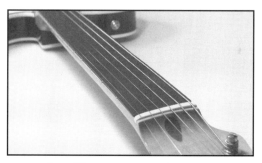

FIGURE 2.11 Fretguards will prevent any damage to your frets from an impact on the guitar case. The fretguard slides between the frets and the strings, protecting the frets from the strings cutting into them during an impact. (Photo by John LeVan)

ATA®-certified cases are approved for air travel. They are generally made from plywood, metal or ABS® plastic. Even with an ATA® certified case, it is important that the guitar does not move freely within the case. If it does move, I recommend using a towel or foam rubber to secure the guitar within the case.

Always store peripheral items such as a tuner, capo and string cutters, etc. in the middle compartment of the case. No good has come from a pair of string cutters bouncing off of your guitar while in transit.

If you must store your guitar for any length of time, it needs to be in a consistent environment. That means the temperature and humidity should not fluctuate much more than 10 degrees and 10 percent humidity. Seventy to 80 degrees

Fahrenheit is relatively safe, and 40 to 50 percent humidity is best. Again it's a good idea to detune your guitar a whole step down (from standard pitch).

Humidity and Temperature

Humidity is the amount of moisture in the air. Too much or too little humidity can make you guitar sound, play and look very bad. Forty to 50 percent is the ideal amount of humidity for a guitar. If a guitar is left in an environment that is too hot or too cold, (like the trunk of a car on a hot day) the result can be devastating. It only takes a few hours of heat to melt the glue that holds your guitar together. Acoustic instruments are affected more often than electric guitars because they are made from thinner pieces of wood and are under more stress and tension. However all instruments need a consistent environment. Here is a list of problems that occur as a result of extremely low humidity:

- Structural Cracks (bridge, neck, top, back, sides)
- Sharp Fret Ends (caused by the fretboard shrinking)
- Warped Neck
- Loose Braces
- Glue Failure
- Cracked Finish (finish checking)
- String Rattle
- Intonation and Tuning Problems

How to Gauge Humidity

There are several products on the market to help you identify the humidity level in your environment. I recommend a digital one that measures both temperature and humidity. Most hardware stores as well as home improvement stores stock them, they retail from $14 to $30. Regardless of which one you choose, consider it to be a very cheap insurance policy for your guitar.

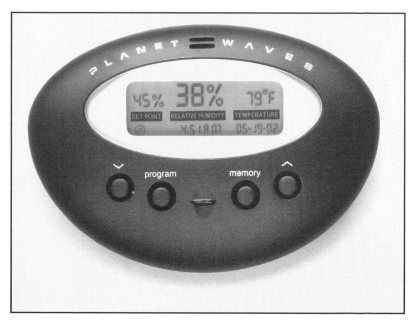

FIGURE 2.12 Most hygrometers will show both the temperature and humidity. (Photo provided by J. D'addario & Co®.)

How to Control Humidity

There are two types of humidifiers that I recommend depending upon where and how your guitar is stored. If your guitar is outside of the case, I recommend a warm-mist room humidifier. Used with your hygrometer (humidity gauge), this method will be quite sufficient. If your guitar is kept inside the case, I recommend either the "Damp-it®" or the "Planet Waves®" humidifier. Either of these humidifiers can be found in most music stores for between $12 and $16. It is still important to use a hygrometer to measure the humidity wherever your guitar is stored.

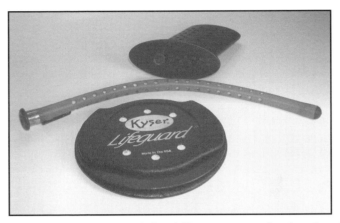

FIGURE 2.13 Here are a few of the different types of guitar humidifiers available. (Photo by John LeVan)

Summary

To prolong the life of your guitar, here is what you need to remember:

1. **Hygiene** (wash up before you play, wipe down the strings when finished playing)

2. **Clean and condition your guitar** (0000 steel wool, lemon oil and guitar polish)

3. **Restring** (strings should last about 20 to 30 playing hours if you keep them clean)

4. **Humidity and temperature** (keep you guitar in a consistent environment)

This guide will help prevent premature wear and tear on your guitar and hopefully reduce costly visits to the repair shop.

Adjusting the Neck

This is the first step in a setup. It is a critical part of the entire process because, if it is done incorrectly, you will have to repeat the following steps in the setup procedure. Chapters 3 thru 7 outline the procedure for doing a setup.

List of Components

The neck has several important components such as:

1. Headstock (can be a multitude of shapes and sizes)

2. Tuning Keys (various colors and styles)

3. Trussrod Cover (not found on all guitars)

4. Trussrod Nut (this can be found at either end of the neck in different guitars)

5. String Nut (can be bone, metal, ivory, wood or plastic)

6. Fretboard (made of ebony, rosewood, maple, micarda or graphite)

7. Frets (nickel, silver and zinc alloy)

8. Trussrod (single action, double action or K-bar)

9. Trussrod anchor (this can be found at either end of the neck in different guitars)

10. Neck Slab (maple, rosewood, graphite or mahogany)

11. Heel (where the neck attaches to the body)

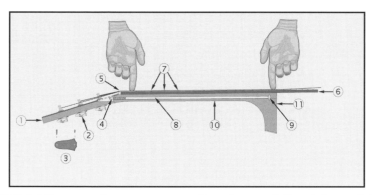

FIGURE 3.1 Here are the components of a guitar neck listed above. (Photo provided by the Taylor Guitar® Company.)

An important aspect of guitar repair is the way in which you record measurements. The measurements you record will help you see the corrections you make as you work on your instrument. Throughout this book we will be recording many different measurements in order to compare the guitar before and after it has been setup. Here are a few foolproof techniques for sighting and adjusting the neck.

To measure the amount of relief (bow) in a neck

1. Tune the guitar to whatever pitch the player will be using

2. Place a capo on top of the first fret over the strings

3. Hold the guitar in playing position

4. Press down low E at the last fret

5. Use your precision scale (ruler) or Action Gauge to measure the distance from the top of the frets to the bottom of the low E string at the middle of the neck

6. Record the largest distance between the frets and string

The first step in setting up any guitar is adjusting the neck. This step is critical because if the neck has too much forebow and you adjust the action at the nut, you will need to replace the nut after you readjust the neck properly. The same is probable if you adjust the action at the bridge (on an acoustic guitar) before adjusting the neck. Unnecessarily replacing parts should be avoided. **The goal is to be accurate, efficient and effective.**

Repeating steps will just waste time and energy. Before sighting the neck, make sure that the guitar is tuned to "concert pitch" (A-440) or whatever tuning the player will be using. Next, sight the neck to check for either a backbow (convex) or a forebow (concave).

There are three basic methods to sight a neck.

1. Visually looking down the neck from the headstock.
2. Holding down the low E string at the 1st and 22nd fret.
3. Setting a straight edge on top of the fingerboard.

Method No. 1 is great if you just want to "eyeball" the neck. However, it isn't very accurate for taking measurements. This technique will help you make a quick judgment as to whether the neck is fore-bowed or back-bowed.

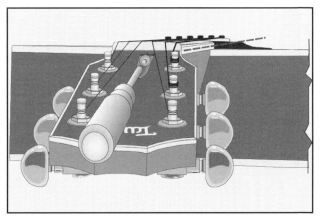

FIGURE 3.2 Holding the neck at the headstock, look down the fretboard to determine if the neck is fore-bowed or back-bowed. (Photo provided by the Taylor Guitar® Company)

Method No. 2 is the easiest way to record an accurate measurement as long as the low E string is in good condition. *If it is bent or dented, your measurement will be inaccurate.* By placing a capo at the first fret and holding the low E string down at the last fret, you can determine just how much forebow a neck has. If the neck is back-bowed, then you will not be able to record any measurements using this method.

FIGURE 3.3A Note that the capo must be on top of the first fret, not in front of or behind it. (Photo by John LeVan)

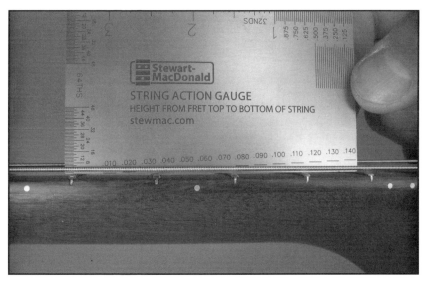

3.3B Hold the low E string down at the last fret and measure the farthest distance between the top of the fret to the bottom of the low E string. (Photo by John LeVan)

Method No. 3 is also a good technique to use when measuring the amount of relief in a neck. Even if the neck is *back-bowed* you can still measure the amount of backbow by holding the straight edge on top of the frets and measuring the distance between the bottom of the straight edge and the *top of the first (or last) fret*. The greater distance should be recorded. If the neck has a *forebow,* then hold the straight edge on top of the frets and measure the distance from the bottom of the straight edge to the *top of the frets in the middle of the neck.*

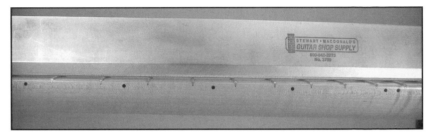

FIGURE 3.4 Method No. 3 is the same concept as method No. 2, however you are substituting the low E string with the straight edge. When using method No. 3, be sure to place the straight edge between the D and G strings onto the top of the frets. As always, record the greatest distance between the top of the frets and the bottom of the straight edge. (Photo by John LeVan)

The Trussrod.

Inside the neck is a trussrod. To adjust the neck, tighten or loosen the trussrod. By tightening the trussrod you force it to straighten or even backbow. When you loosen the trussrod, it releases the pressure and forebows or becomes concave. Turning the trussrod clockwise will tighten and counter-clockwise will loosen it. If the neck is back-bowed, then loosen the rod. If the neck is fore-bowed, tighten the rod. **[When working on a vintage or old guitar you should always loosen the strings before tightening the trussrod].** If you don't you risk stripping the rod and that's an expensive repair! **When in doubt, consult with a qualified luthier.**

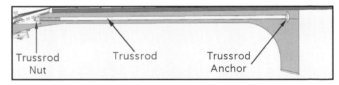

FIGURE 3.5 Here is a diagram of a trussrod, trussrod nut, and anchor. (Photo provided by the Taylor Guitar® Company)

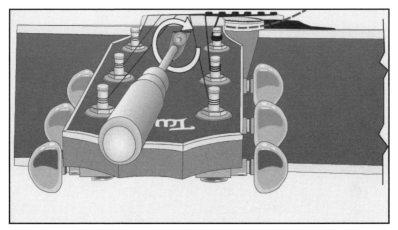

FIGURE 3.6 Here is a neck with too much forebow or too much relief in it. The trussrod needs to be tightened by turning it clockwise. (Photo provided by the Taylor Guitar® Company)

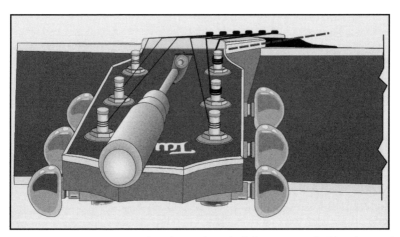

FIGURE 3.7 Here is a correctly adjusted neck. (Photo provided by the Taylor Guitar® Company)

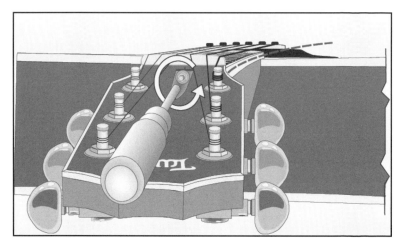

FIGURE 3.8 Here is a neck that is convex or back-bowed. The trussrod needs to be loosened by turning it counter-clockwise. (Photo provided by the Taylor Guitar® Company)

Most trussrod adjustments require a hex key, screwdriver or a nut driver (socket wrench). See illustrations above. There should be a slight amount of forebow in the neck, (approximately .010" to .015") dependent upon the instrument and condition of the neck. If the player wants fast and low action, .010" of relief is plenty. If the player uses a capo or is heavy handed, then .015" or more is recommended.

We will discuss neck adjustments in depth in this book. *The object of the exercise is to adjust the guitar to the player.* Knowing the style and technique of the player is critical to properly adjusting the guitar. Everyone has his or her own style and technique; that's why it's important to match the setup to the player.

There are two types of trussrods, adjustable and non-adjustable. Non-adjustable are also called K-bars or steel-reinforced rods. Adjustable trussrods come in two varieties, single and double action.

Single-action trussrods only force the neck in one direction. As you tighten a single-action trussrod, it forces it to straighten or backbow the neck. When you loosen the rod it releases the pressure. These are common in most guitars. A common dilemma is when you have a neck that is back-bowed even after you have completely loosened the trussrod. To correct this you either have to replace the trussrod or plane and re-fret the neck. Both repairs are expensive and require an experienced luthier.

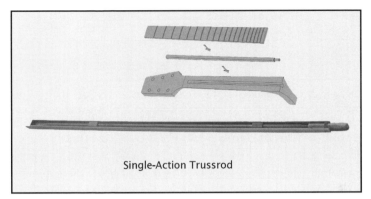

Single-Action Trussrod

FIGURE 3.9 Single action trussrods are common in most modern guitars. This type of trussrod will only force the neck in one direction. (Illustration by John LeVan)

Double-action trussrods force the neck in both directions. If the trussrod is loose and the neck is still back-bowed, then keep turning it until it forces the neck in the other direction. These trussrods are more stable and are usually found in finer guitars and basses.

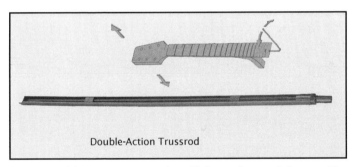

Double-Action Trussrod

FIGURE 3.10 Double-action trussrods will force the neck in two directions, thus making it easier to do setups and fretwork. (Illustration by John LeVan)

Troubleshooting

As I mentioned earlier, trussrod repairs are difficult and expensive. In many cases it is more cost effective to buy a new neck than it is to repair a broken trussrod. There are several things that can go wrong with a trussrod. They can freeze or rust, break, strip and cause the neck and fretboard to separate. Here are a few tips to identify a damaged trussrod:

- It spins freely when tightening
- It will not turn in either direction
- Rattles inside the neck when you play
- Has been run over by a car!

Occasionally, the only damage is the trussrod nut has stripped. If this is the case, then simply replace it and you're back in business. A new trussrod nut is about $2. Whatever the case may be, if you are unsure, ask a professional. There is no substitute for experience, and nothing builds confidence like the experiences you will gain with time.

If the trussrod will not tighten, back off the trussrod nut and check to see if either the nut or rod is stripped. If the nut is stripped, replace it. If the rod is stripped, take it to a qualified luthier.

Adjusting the Action at the Bridge

Adjusting the action at the bridge is step two in the setup process. We adjust the string height at the bridge in order to make it easier to play the higher notes on the neck of the guitar. So far, we have done step one (adjusted the neck), and now step two (adjust the height of the bridge).

List of Components

* Tunematic®
* Tremolo Systems
* Hardtail

FIGURE 4.1 Tunematic® bridges are found on some electric guitars. They comprise of a bridge base, bridge saddles, intonation adjustment screws, retention spring or wire, threaded inserts for the thumbwheels and thumbwheels for height adjustment. (Photo by John LeVan)

FIGURE 4.2A There are several types of tremolo systems on the market. The most common are fulcrum style, single- and double-locking and bigsby style. (Photo by John LeVan)

FIGURE 4.2B They are composed of a base, tremolo arm (whammy bar), bridge saddles, saddle height adjustment screws, intonation adjustment screws, saddle locking screws, fine tuners, spring plate, inertia block and tremolo arm spring. (Photo provided by L.R. Baggs®)

FIGURE 4.2C Notice that not all of these systems use the same components. (Photo by John LeVan)

FIGURE 4.3 Hardtail bridges are common on Tele® style, electric guitars. Occasionally they are also found on Strat® style guitars as well. Hardtail refers to the fact that they are attached flush to the body and aren't a tremolo. These bridges are made up of bridge saddles, saddle height adjustment screws, intonation screws and springs, bridge plate and string ferrells. (Photo by John LeVan)

The player's style is the deciding factor on an absolute height to follow. The strings should consistently graduate at least 1/64" from high E to low E. This will compensate for the difference in thickness in the strings. If every string were the same height, either the treble strings would be too high or the bass strings would tend to rattle.

Adjusting the action at the bridge can be done several ways depending upon the instrument. An electric guitar can be corrected by adjusting a thumbwheel or an Allen-screw. If it is an acoustic guitar, it is generally adjusted by sanding the bottom of the bridge saddle. One of the most important elements of a good setup is adjusting the guitar for the player's particular style. If the player is heavy handed, the action (or distance of the strings to the frets) needs to be higher, if light handed then the action can be lower. If the action is too high, then the guitar can be difficult to play and can cause intonation problems. If too low, it can cause string rattle and dead spots on the string.

Measuring the Action at the Bridge

1. I recommend a well-machined scale (ruler) or Action Gauge® with good contrast that will measure to 1/64".

2. Place a capo over the strings on top of the first fret.

3. Measure the distance from the top of the 12th fret to the bottom of each string.

4. Record your measurements.

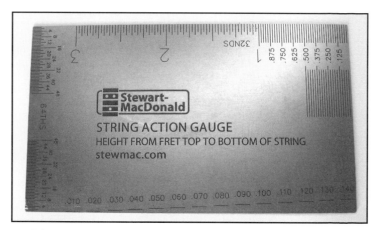

FIGURE 4.4 A good scale (rule) to use is one that is 1/4" x up to 6", with sharp contrast which makes it easy to read. The Stewart-MacDonald® Action Gauge® is an excellent tool. (Photo by John LeVan)

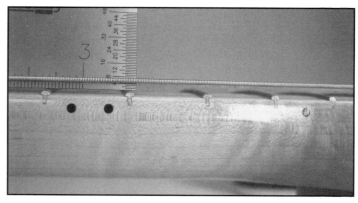

FIGURE 4.5 When measuring the action at the 12th fret, make sure your scale is level when you place it on top of the fret. It is also helpful to have a lot of light on the subject so that you can clearly see the measurements. (Photo by John LeVan)

Start with the high E and work your way to the low E. After you record the measurements for each string adjust the action of each string to the desired height. Keep in mind that you'll need to set the low E string approximately 1/64" higher than the high E string. All the other strings will graduate somewhere in between. The B string will be slightly higher than the high E, the G string will be slightly higher than the B string, etc.

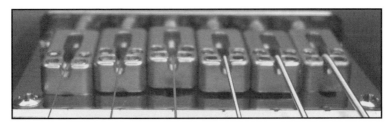

FIGURE 4.6 A gradual increase in the height of each string is the goal. If you raise the action too much, the guitar will be difficult to play; too little, and it will rattle and buzz. (Photo by John LeVan)

From time to time, you will encounter a guitar with a Tunematic® bridge, (Les Paul® or SG® type) that has inconsistent string height and incorrect string spacing. In this case, it is recommended that you either re-cut the saddles (using nut files) or replace the bridge all together. If the bridge looks as though it is sinking in the middle, it needs to be replaced.

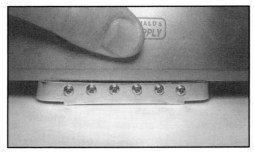

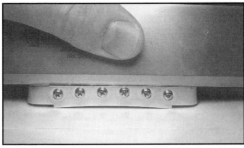

FIGURE 4.7A & 4.7B Note the difference between a sinking bridge and a good bridge. This is a common problem with this style of bridge. Also, the spacing on the sinking bridge is inconsistent while the good bridge has accurate string spacing. Accurate spacing will make the guitar easier to play. (Photo by John LeVan)

To adjust a Strat®, Tele® style or bass bridge, use a hex key set. The sizes can differ for each guitar from .05" to 1.5mm, but the basics remain the same. Remember that it is important to make sure that the saddle is level after you adjust it. Like all skills, practice makes perfect. To raise the saddle, turn the hex screw clockwise. To lower the saddle, turn the hex screw counter clockwise.

FIGURE 4.8 These types of saddles are adjusted by two hex screws. It is important to keep them level with the bridge plate. It may play ok, but if they aren't level your setup will not look very professional. (Photo by John LeVan)

To adjust a tremolo style bridge, you may need hex keys, Phillips-head or flat-head screwdrivers. Make sure to know whether to adjust the tremolo flush or with a certain amount of "draw." "Draw" refers to the increments of notes you can pull sharp using the tremolo bar. Some players prefer a flush mount bridge for doing double-stop bends, etc. Some prefer a half–to–whole-note draw to accent a solo or chord. Adjusting the tremolo springs in the back of the guitar does this. The tremolo springs are adjusted by, (tightening and loosening) the screws on the claw. With each adjustment, tune the guitar to pitch and retest the amount of draw. To adjust the tremolo flush to the body, tighten the screws on the claw. To float the tremolo, loosen the screws on the claw. This may take several attempts to get it right. **IT IS VERY IMPORTANT TO RETUNE THE GUITAR TO THE CORRECT PITCH EACH TIME YOU MAKE AN ADJUSTMENT**. Otherwise, you will end up with the tremolo that is positioned forward (un-level) rendering the guitar unplayable.

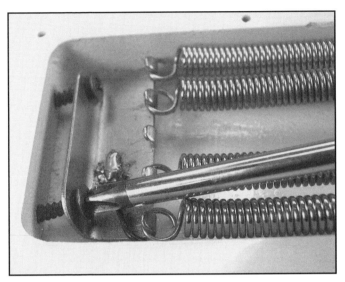

FIGURE 4.9 Regardless of what tool you need to adjust this type of bridge, it's important that you set it up to accommodate the player's style. Whether the player wants to draw the bridge back, or will never use the whammy bar, make sure that the spring claw is adjusted for that style of play. (Photo by John LeVan)

Neck angle issues can really complicate matters and apply to all guitars. In this example, we are using a guitar with a tremolo system. Here is a list of possible symptoms of an incorrect neck angle:

FIGURE 4.10 Tremolo is flush to body, bridge saddles are adjusted as high as possible, but action is still too low. (Photo by John LeVan)

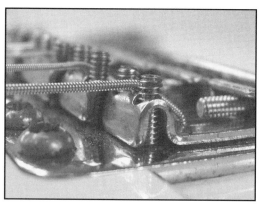

FIGURE 4.11 Tremolo is flush to body, bridge saddles are adjusted as low as possible, but action is too high. (Photo by John LeVan)

To correct this problem on an electric is fairly simple. Place an angled shim under the neck to tilt it to the correct angle. It is critically important to use a shim that is the same size as the neck pocket. Just throwing a pick under the neck is not a good idea because it can cause the neck to warp where it bolts onto the body. As for an acoustic guitar, unless it has a bolt-on neck, changing the neck angle is time consuming and expensive. Only a qualified, factory-authorized luthier should attempt this.

FIGURE 4.12 If the shim doesn't fully cover the pocket, it can result in tone loss and neck warping. (Photo by John LeVan)

Adjusting the Action at the Nut

Adjusting the action at the nut is step three of a setup. This is a very important part of the setup because if the action is too high at the nut, the guitar will be difficult to play and will not play in tune. High action at the nut is usually only needed when the player is using a slide.

So far we have done step one (adjusting the neck), step two (adjusting the action at the bridge), and now step three (adjusting the action at the nut).

List of Components

String Nut

- String Slots
- String Angles
- Slot Width
- String Spacing
- Precision Scale/Rule

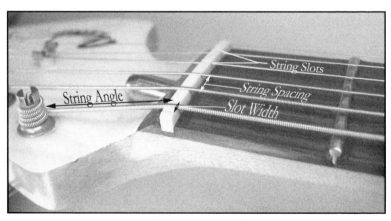

FIGURE 5.1 Here is a photo of the string nut. (Photo by John LeVan)

Tools Needed:

- Nut Files
- Scale (Miniature Metal Ruler)

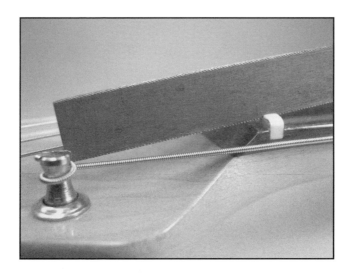

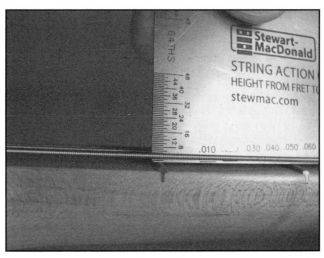

FIGURE 5.2A & FIGURE 5.2B Nut files and a scale are essential to do this project properly. Make sure to choose the correct nut files for the guitar you are working on, and in particular, for the gauge of strings being used on it. (Photo by John LeVan)

A proven way to adjust the string height at the nut is to use a set of nut files. I recommend at least 10 different sizes:

- .010
- .012
- .016
- .022
- .026
- .032
- .036
- .040
- .046
- .052

Angles, Width and Spacing

It is critically important to cut the slot at the correct angle, width and spacing. The *angle* of the slot should match the angle of the string from the front of the nut to the tuning key peg. If the slot angle is incorrect, then the string will either rattle or not intonate properly. If the string slot is not cut to the proper width, then it can cause tuning problems, string breakage and string rattle. The *width* of the slot is equally important. When the slot is too narrow the string will bind in the slot and can break as well as cause tuning problems. If the slot is cut too wide, the string will rattle and buzz when played in the open position. String *spacing* is the distance from one string to another. If there is a greater space between the B and G string than between the A and low E string, then the spacing is incorrect. This can make the guitar difficult to play. Each string should be the same distance from the next. Measuring from the outside edge of the strings, all the strings should be the same distance from each other.

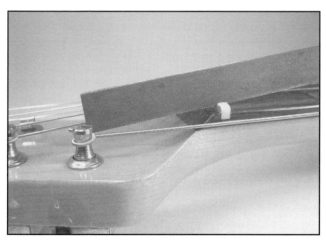

FIGURE 5.3 Be sure to cut the string slot at the same angle as the string from the face of the nut to the end of the tuning key peg. (Photo by John LeVan)

Never cut the slot more that 2/1000" over the width of the string. Equally as important is to avoid cutting the slot too narrow.

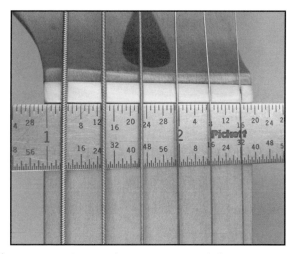

FIGURE 5.4 String spacing is also important. If the spacing is off, it can cause the E strings to slip off of the neck when you play. (Photo by John LeVan)

Proper Adjustments

All proper adjustment begins with accurate measurements.

To measure action at the nut, tune the guitar to pitch, and place your rule on top of the first fret at the high E string. Record the distance from the top of the fret to the bottom of the string. Generally you need about 1/64" or 15/1000" distance from the top of the fret to the bottom of the string for the high E string. For the low E string double the distance. *Keep in mind that the actual height will ultimately be determined by the player's style. If the player is heavy handed, you need to add about .010" of height.* **The low E should be slightly higher than the high E by at least 1/64".** The rest of the strings should be an ascending balance between the two E strings. In other words, the B string will be slightly higher than the high E string, the G will be slightly higher than the B string, etc. **It may take a while to train your eye to see such small detail, but like all skills, practice makes perfect. This is the same formula used in Chapter 4 on adjusting the action at the bridge.**

Replacement and Repair

There are times when you just need a quick fix, and there are times when you need a permanent repair. A quick fix is acceptable when you're on the road or don't have the time and resources for a permanent repair. Filling the nut is a quick fix and a temporary repair. You should replace the nut as soon as possible if it's worn or cut too low. Below are some common problems and some quick fixes and permanent solutions.

When the string slot is cut too low. The strings will rattle on the open notes often called the *sitar effect.* There are two ways to fix this problem.

1. Fill the string slot with a material that is the same as what the nut is made of

2. Replace the nut

If you don't have the resources to replace the nut, then the next best thing is to fill the slot and re-cut it. This is only a temporary fix until you can replace it.

To Repair / Fill Nut Slot

- Clean out the slot removing any dirt, graphite or glue

- Then fill slot with either bone or plastic dust [whatever material the nut is made of]

- Add a drop of Super Glue® to seal and bond the dust into the slot

- Spray Super Glue® Accelerator onto slot (glue will dry immediately)

- Re-cut the slot to the correct depth

FIGURE 5.5 Clean out the slot using a nut file. You may want to use a file that is slightly larger than the slot for this. (Photo by John LeVan)

FIGURE 5.6 Loosely pack the slot with a like material to the nut. If the nut is bone, use bone. (Photo by John LeVan)

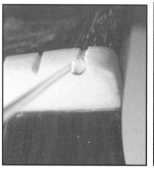

FIGURE 5.7A,B Apply one drop of thin Super Glue® to the slot. Always have a Q-Tip® in your hand when working with Super Glue®. Use the Q-Tip® to absorb any excess glue before it can drip onto the finish. (Photo by John LeVan)

Spray a little bit of Super Glue® accelerator into the slot to speed up the drying process.

FIGURE 5.8 Re-cut the string slot to the correct width, depth and angle. (Photo by John LeVan)

To replace the nut, use a flathead screwdriver and lightly tap the front of the nut with the tip of the screwdriver to break it loose. If this isn't working try a drop of solvent. *Make sure you don't get any of the solvent on the finish of the neck. Solvent can melt the finish of most guitars.* Then clean out the nut slot with a miniature file to remove all the glue before you install the new nut. Be certain that the nut fits snug and flush. Using a drop of thin Super Glue® between the A and D string, secure it to the end of the fingerboard. Re-cut the string slots to the proper action as per the instructions at the beginning of this chapter.

Adjusting the Pickups

Adjusting the pickups is step four of a setup. If done properly, your pickups will sound full and balanced. If done incorrectly, your guitar will sound unbalanced and can develop string rattle and intonation problems. At this point you should have completed step one (adjusting the trussrod), step two (adjusting the bridge), step three (adjusting the nut) and now step four (adjusting the pickups).

List of Components:

- Pickups
- Strings
- Pickup Height Adjustment Screws

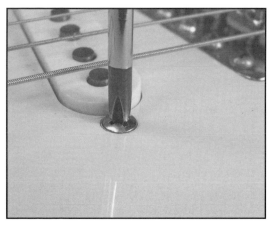

FIGURE 6.1, The screws on each side of the pickup are used to adjust its height in relationship to the strings. (Photo by John LeVan)

Proper Height and Effects

The purpose of adjusting the pickups is to ensure an even volume for each string. It can also minimize fret buzz and intonation problems. *This is primarily done on magnetic pickups only.* Pickup adjustment is done by changing the height of the pickup, in relationship to the strings. If the pickup height is too high, it can cause string buzz and intonation problems due to the magnetic pull of the pickup on the strings. If the pickups are too low, it causes a weak signal and unbalanced string volume.

Proper adjustment is dependent upon the height of the pickup in relationship to the string. Generally, the bridge pickup can be closer to the string than the other pickups. This is because that location of the string is least likely to be pulled out of intonation by the magnets in the pickups. The strings are not as stable at the middle and neck positions.

Pickup height can vary from 3/32" to 6/32" from pickup to pickup. I generally set the **pickup** at 3/32" at the **treble side** and 4/32" at the **bass side.** I don't recommend setting the pickups any higher than this because it can cause the magnetic poles on the pickup to pull on the string. The most accurate way to measure the pickup height is to hold the string down at the last fret and measure the string at the pickup on the high and low E strings. From there, test the string balance by playing the guitar and listening to the volume of each string from pickup to pickup, adjusting the height of the pickups accordingly.

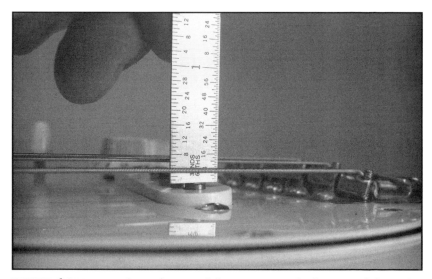

FIGURE 6.2 Measure from the top of the magnet to the bottom of the string (while you hold the strings down at the last fret). (Photo by John LeVan)

Setting the Intonation

Setting the intonation is step five of a setup. Without setting the intonation, the guitar will never play, even close to, in tune. So far we have completed step one (adjusting the neck), step two (adjusting the action at the bridge), step three (adjusting the action at the nut), step four (adjusting the pickups) and now step five (setting the intonation).

Intonation means to be in perfect unison. The purpose for intonating a guitar is so that it plays in tune both with itself and with other properly intonated instruments. Understanding the fundamentals and variables of intonation is crucial to the performance of any guitar. Even the best guitars are useless if they don't play in tune. Learning to intonate and temper an instrument are skills that you will learn in this chapter. We will define, test and discuss variables and temperaments and how to balance them to the instrument as well as the player.

Tools Needed

There are many different types of guitar bridges. Therefore, you will need several types of tools including:

- Hex Keys
- Flathead Screwdrivers
- Phillips-Head Screwdrivers

As discussed in Chapter 4, most electric guitar bridges are adjusted with either a screwdriver or hex keys. The screw or hex bolt in the rear of the bridge allows you to adjust the bridge saddle back and forth. Changing the position of the bridge saddle will change the intonation of the instrument.

Testing

Before you set the intonation, be sure that the following four steps have been completed in order:

1. Adjust the neck
2. Adjust the action at the bridge
3. Adjust the action at the nut
4. Adjust the pickups (where applicable)

Once the guitar is in tune (using a guitar tuner) and the strings are settled and holding their tune, then check the **12th fret harmonic** against the fretted-note at the 12th fret on each string. Make sure that you read the ***attack*** of the note not the ***drift*** when using your tuner. The ***attack*** is the immediate reaction of the note; ***drift*** is where the note settles. The goal is to match the harmonic tone with the fretted note. **The harmonic is always true, so that is your constant or control note. The fretted note is always the variable.** It is very important to use an accurate tuner for adjusting the intonation. A Saunderson Accutuner® or a Strobe tuner are the best type on the market at present time.

Sharp, Flat and Hopeless? Now that you have established whether the fretted note is either sharp (♯) or flat (♭), it's time to adjust the intonation for each saddle. If the fretted note is sharp (♯) then the saddle for that string needs to be moved away from the neck (back). If the fretted note is flat (♭) then the saddle needs to move towards the neck (forward). **Sharp** (♯) means the string is too **short; flat** (♭) means the string is too **long.**

FIGURE 7.1 On an electric guitar, tighten the intonation screw if the note is sharp (♯). If the note is flat (♭) loosen the screw. (Photo by John LeVan)

Variables and tempering need to be identified and understood in order to control them. A critical variable to intonating is the string nut. If the front of the nut is worn or chipped, it can cause the intonation to be sharp ($\sharp$). This is why intonating is the last step in a setup.

Other variables include:

- Worn Frets
- Inaccurate Fret Placement
- Inaccurate Nut Placement
- Inaccurate Bridge Saddle Placement
- Pick Size
- Velocity of Strum
- Fret Height
- How Hard You Press the String Down

One of the most widely used calculations to determine nut, fret and saddle placement is the *Rule of 18*. The Rule of 18 is rather complicated, however, if the placement of the above listed components are not correct, the guitar will never play well in tune. Six out of seven of the above listed variables are correctable, fret placement is not cost effective to correct. However, there are adjustments that can be made to offset this common problem.

Believe it or not, no instrument can play perfectly in tune. Thus, the art of *tempering* was developed. Tempering is the balancing of tones to make an instrument sound more pleasing to the ear. In other words, each string on a guitar is intonated and tuned slightly off pitch in order to make most chords sound in tune. The piano is commonly temper-tuned in order to play in tune with itself. Likewise, a guitar can also be temper-tuned. This practice dates back to the time of Bach when he nearly lost his head because he subverted tradition by temper-tuning his piano. By adjusting the intonation screws on the bridge saddles (on most guitars), you can easily temper it to sound more pleasing.

As far as the electric guitars go, the G string is the biggest problem - compounded by the high E string. Keep in mind we are talking about a guitar with a plain G string, not a wound G string. For a guitar with a plain G string, I intonate all but the high E and G at the 12th fret. Intonate the high E at the 3rd fret like the low E on an acoustic. Then I play the G string at the 15th fret and compare it with the open D string. I then intonate (adjust the length of the string), the G **by ear** (sounds frightening huh?) until it sounds in tune with the open A and D strings. I don't use a guitar tuner for intonating the G string because, even though the tuner shows that the G is intonated, it won't sound in tune on several of the commonly played chords. **Make sure you retune after every adjustment**. I know it sounds complicated, but this is the best system I have found without making permanent modifications (like relocating the string nut or the bridge) to the instrument.

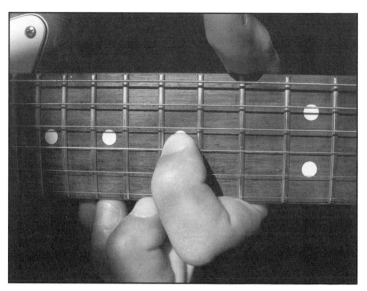

FIGURE 7.2 After tuning the guitar to the desired pitch, fret the G string at the 15th fret and check to see if the note is in tune with the open A and D strings. Then adjust the saddle as needed. (Photo by John LeVan)

This completes the setup process. At this point we have completed step one (adjusting the neck), step two (adjusting the action at the bridge), step three (adjusting the action at the nut), step four (adjusting the pickups) and finally, step five (setting the intonation). Your guitar should now play better than ever, and who knows? Maybe someday you'll be a rock star!

Top 10 Signs of a Problematic Guitar

Before you purchase an instrument, make sure that you completely inspect it before you buy it. It is always a good idea to bring along someone who can identify serious problems and defects when you shop for an instrument. Many repair shops offer an "evaluation" or "inspection" for a small fee. It's better to pay $20 or $30 to find a serious problem before you buy, than to spend over a $1,000 on an instrument that needs an overhaul.

Electric Guitar

1. Won't play in tune

2. Worn string nut

3. Fret wear

4. Bad neck angle

5. Electronics malfunction

6. Cracked or stripped bridge saddles

7. Loose or uneven frets

8. Uneven fretboard

9. Broken trussrod

10. Broken headstock

FIGURE 8.1 Frets become flat and develop an almost diamond-shaped dent as they wear. (Photo by John LeVan)

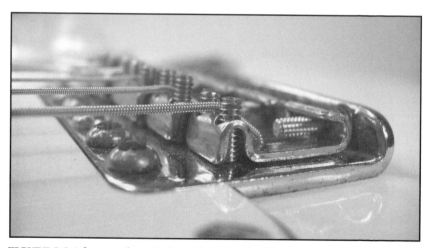

FIGURE 8.2 A low neck angle is easily identified because the guitar will have high action even if the bridge and saddles are as low as they can go. (Photo by John LeVan)

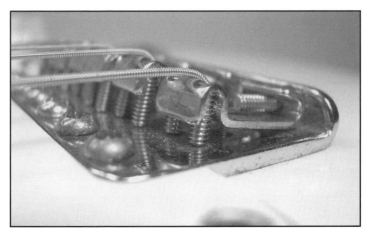

FIGURE 8.3 A high neck angle is easily identified because the guitar will have very low action even if the bridge and saddles are as high as they can go. (Photo by John LeVan)

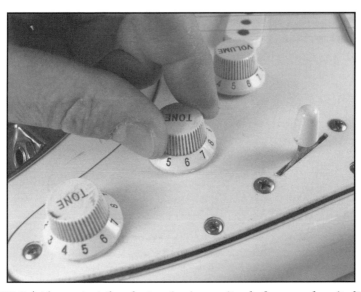

FIGURE 8.4 Always test the electronics in a guitar before you buy it. (Photo by John LeVan)

FIGURE 8.5 Inspect the hardware and make sure it isn't rusted, chipped or cracked. (Photo by John LeVan)

FIGURE 8.6 Make sure that the frets haven't separated from the fretboard, this can very expensive to repair. (Photo by John LeVan)

If the fretboard is wavy or looks uneven, it probably needs a plane and re-fret.

Broken trussrods are detected by adjusting them and then checking the results.

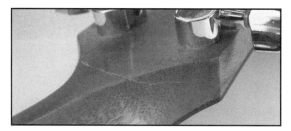

FIGURE 8.7 Look carefully for any sign of a crack or a repaired crack. Even though a properly repaired headstock will last decades, the fact that it was broken de-values the guitar by as much as 50 percent. (Photo by John LeVan)

With the information discussed in the previous chapters of this book, you should be able to identify each of these problems by thoroughly inspecting the instrument you are considering. Many of these ailments are very expensive to repair, so be very attentive and meticulous when you conduct your inspection.

Other Upgrades and Repairs

There are several ways to upgrade and improve your guitar's performance without detracting from its value. Below are a few examples of how to upgrade your instrument.

Tuning Keys

List of Components

- Headstock
- Tuning Keys
- Mounting Screws
- Tuning Key Hole
- Tuning Key Button
- Tuning Key Post
- Screw-in Collar
- Press-in Collar

The quality of your tuning keys will make a big difference in respect to your guitar's ability to stay in tune. The higher the turning ratio, the better it will tune. In other words, the more times you have to turn the button to achieve one revolution of the tuning key post, the finer the tuning. The turning ratio of most tuning keys will range from 11:1 to 18:1. 11:1 to 14:1 is a terrible turning ratio. 15:1 up to 16:1 is a good turning ratio. 18:1 and up, is an excellent turning ratio.

Matching the correct key to your guitar is important. There are many different types of keys on the market. Whether your guitar has a set of vintage keys or the latest locking keys, chances are you will find a set that will be an exact retrofit for your guitar. I recommend that you only use keys that are an exact retrofit so that you don't have to alter the guitar to install them. Altering a guitar to replace the keys will adversely affect the value of a guitar. Brands like Gotoh® and Schaller® offer a wide range of tuning keys with good to excellent turning ratios and affordable prices. They range in price from $35 up to $125.

Tuning Key Installation

There are a few basic tools needed to replace tuning keys.

Tool List

- Cordless Drill with Small-Tip Phillips-head
- 10mm Deep-Well Socket (optional)
- Knob Puller (optional)

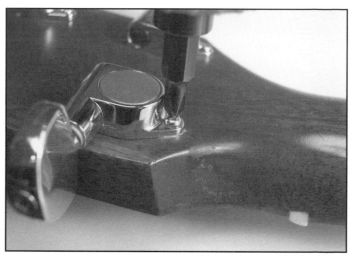

FIGURE 9.1 Small Phillips-head tip along with your cordless drill is perfect to remove the tuning key screws that hold the keys to the headstock. (Photo by John LeVan)

FIGURE 9.2 A 10mm deep-well socket is the perfect size for most tuning keys with a screw-in collar. If the tuning keys have press-in collars (bushings), you won't need this tool. (Photo by John LeVan)

FIGURE 9.3 A knob puller is only necessary if you need to remove press-in bushings. If the bushings will work with the new keys, don't remove them. If the old bushings are too small, you will need to remove them from the instrument and install the new set provided by the tuning key manufacturer. (Photo by John LeVan)

Keep in mind the risk in removing a press-in bushing. It is very easy to chip or lift the finish around the bushing. Unless absolutely necessary, avoid removing press-in bushings.

Here are the simple steps for removing the tuning keys.

1. Remove the strings from the guitar.

2. Remove the screws holding the tuning keys to the headstock.

3. Remove (if applicable) the threaded collar that surrounds the tuning key post.

4. Slide the tuning keys out of the headstock.

When removing the screws from the tuning keys (on the backside of the headstock), be careful not to strip them. You may want to set your cordless drill on a slower setting.

FIGURE 9.4 If the tuning keys have a screw-in collar, remove it. Not all tuning keys require the same tools when replacing, so make sure you use the right tool for the job. (Photo by John LeVan)

FIGURE 9.5 The tuning keys should slide right out of the peg-holes in the headstock. (Photo by John LeVan)

When installing the new tuning keys, be sure that they match up with the original equipment you have just removed. If the new keys don't fit into the original peg-holes, don't force them. You may not have the right keys.

FIGURE 9.6 If the old keys have press-in bushings that are smaller than the new bushings, you will need to remove the old bushings and install new ones. This is only recommended if absolutely necessary. You risk damaging the finish on the face of the headstock every time you remove one of the bushings. (Photo by John LeVan)

FIGURE 9.7 When installing a tuning key with a threaded collar, do not over tighten the collar. The collar can easily strip, ruining the tuning key. The collar only needs to be "finger" tight. There is no reason to torque it down with excessive pressure. (Photo by John LeVan)

After installing the new tuning keys, re-string the guitar and you're in business. The most important points I can stress to you are:

- Use keys that are an exact retrofit.

- Always use the correct tool for the job.

- Never over-torque a screw or treaded collar.

Bone String Nut

A bone string nut will improve sustain and tone of almost any guitar. Carving one isn't easy. It requires a lot of practice and patience. Here is what you need to get started.

Tool and Materials List

- 100-Grit Sandpaper.
- 220-Grit Sandpaper.
- 1500-Grit Sandpaper.

- Flat Surface.
- Nut File Set.
- Needle File Set.
- Mechanical Pencil.
- Thin Super Glue®.
- Super Glue® Accelerator.
- Q-Tips®.
- Magnifying Lamp.
- Scale (rule).
- Fretting Hammer.
- Flathead Screwdriver.
- Bone Blank.

Before you start, make sure that you have a good piece of bone to start with. If it is porous, cracked or too oily, you may have problems with it functioning properly as a string nut. Here are step-by-step instructions on carving a new string nut.

1. Remove the old nut (see Chapter 5) with a flathead screwdriver and a fretting hammer.

2. Clean out the nut slot (see Chapter 5) using your needle files.

3. Sand the nut blank to the proper width. Use the 100-grit paper to remove a lot of material and the 220-grit paper to remove just a little. The 1500-grit paper is to polish the nut blank. Make sure that the blank fits squarely into the slot, without any gaps. The blank should fit into the slot snug.

4. Mark the edges of the nut blank with your mechanical pencil to show how much material you need remove to make it flush with the sides of the fretboard.

5. Sand one side of the nut blank, first with 220-grit, then with 1500-grit sandpaper until it is flush with the fretboard.

6. Repeat Step 5 on the other side of the nut blank.

7. Lay your scale (rule) flat on top of the frets with the edge against the face of the nut blank. Mark the blank with your pencil along the scale from the treble side to the bass side of the blank. This is your guide to keep you from carving into the nut too far.

8. Remove the nut blank and sand the top of it down to the pencil line (you may want to leave a little extra material on the bass side). Shape the top of the blank so that it slopes (angles) towards the headstock.

9. Using your magnifying lamp, pencil and your scale (rule), measure out the string spacing on the nut blank. Generally, the two E strings are 1/8" from the edge of the fretboard. Be sure to measure from the outside of the string, not the center of the string. The rest of the strings are generally 1/4" apart (give or take 1/64"). Classical, as well as some steel stringed guitars, have wider string spacing. Make sure that you measure the spacing of the strings on the old nut to get an idea of what the spacing should be for the new one. Next mark the location on the nut blank with your pencil of each string slot to the actual width of that string. The object of the exercise is to place each string the same distance from the other (based on the outside of the string, not the center).

10. Cut the string slots (shallow), now is a good time to install the strings and tune them to pitch.

11. Measure the distance from the edge of the fretboard to the E strings as well as the distance between the strings. Adjust them accordingly and finish cutting the string slots to the proper depth.

12. Remove the strings, secure the nut with a drop of Super Glue® (to the face of the nut), and polish with 1500 grit sandpaper and a polishing cloth.

13. Restring.

FIGURE 9.8 Make sure the nut blank fits in the slot, square and flush. (Photo by John LeVan)

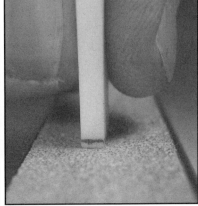

FIGURE 9.9A,B Mark the edge of the blank and adjust the width of the blank one side at a time. (Photo by John LeVan)

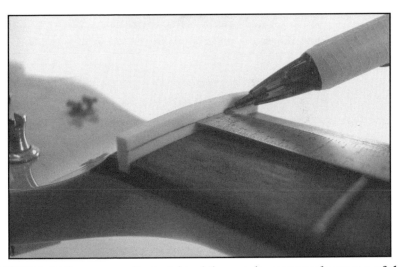

FIGURE 9.10 To measure the height of the nut, lay your scale on top of the frets and mark the face of the nut with a pencil. (Photo by John LeVan)

FIGURE 9.11, Sand the excess material off of the top of the nut blank and reshape. (Photo by John LeVan)

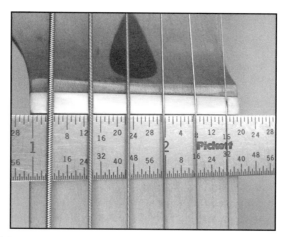

FIGURE 9.12 Measure to proper distance for each string in relationship to the fretboard and each other. (Photo by John LeVan)

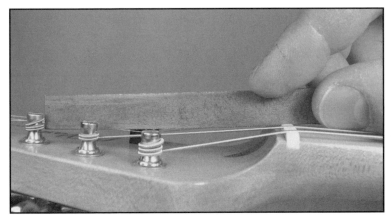

FIGURE 9.13 Carve shallow slots into the nut blank and restring. (Photo by John LeVan)

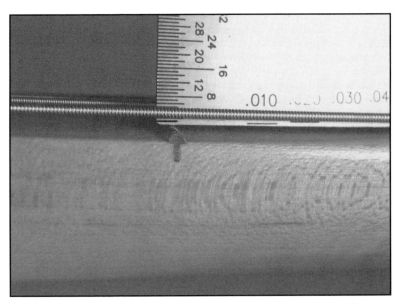

FIGURE 9.14 Shore-up the distances of the slots and cut them to the proper depth and distance. (Photo by John LeVan)

Polish the string nut.

Other Training Resources

There are several sources of training available to aspiring luthiers. Apprenticeships, factory training and workshops are three of the best ways I know to learn and develop old and new skills. I have been fortunate enough to have experienced all three through other repair techs, luthiers, luthier guilds and manufacturers. I recommend these resources to anyone who wants to learn more about this ancient and fascinating trade.

Apprenticeships

The ancient tradition of apprenticeship is still alive and a great way to learn a skill or trade. An apprenticeship begins with the basics; sweeping floors, polishing guitars and taking out the trash. Eventually, you get to watch the master practice his or her craft and ask a few questions. It is best to keep a journal while studying under someone. There are always new questions and deeper answers. The more you learn, the more there is to know. Before you know it, you're in the middle of a neck reset or a bridge reglue on a vintage guitar. An apprenticeship will cost you a lot of time, but it is worth it. You get back what you invest, so invest wisely.

Factory Training

Factory training for me was like working in an emergency room. I was amazed at how fast and accurate these guys worked. I thought I was efficient until I spent some time with the repair techs at the Taylor Guitar® factory. It was a crash course in everything from top replacement to bridge reglues to neck resets. It was an amazing adventure. Factory training is one of the best ways to learn hardcore repair skills.

Workshops

When I lived and worked in Northern California, I was a part of a luthiers guild. We organized workshops and training seminars as well as swap meets. It was a great way to co-op with other luthiers to buy parts, tools and materials at a volume discount. There was always something to teach, learn and rediscover for me at the guild meetings. This is a great way to network with other luthiers to help carry on this great craft.

Glossary

0000 Steel Wool, long, hair-like threads of steel, used for cleaning, polishing and smoothing. 0000 (ultra fine) refers to the grit or cut of the steel wool.

Action, movement of parts or mechanisms. In reference to the guitar, the playability of, and/or the height of the strings in relationship to the fretboard.

Action Gauge®, tool engineered to measure the action of the guitar.

Apprenticeship, period of training, study of a craft.

Attack, velocity of strike; amount of force used to make a sound.

Binding, the wrap or gird around the body and/or neck of an instrument.

Bolt-on Neck, guitar neck that attaches with bolts, instead of glue.

Braces, truss-like supports used to re-enforce the top and back of an acoustic instrument.

Bridge, mechanical or stationary base that holds the strings of a guitar.

Bridge Plate, wooden plate that holds the ball end of a string in place and supports the top of an acoustic instrument under the bridge

Conditioning, saturation and treatment of wood.

Crown, top or peak of a fret.

Cutaway, an area of the upper body on the treble side of a guitar that has been removed or cut away to give the player easier access to the higher notes on the neck.

Cyanoacrylite, transparent, thermoplastic resin containing cyanogens. Super Glue®.

Cyanoacrylite Accelerator, sprayable liquid that accelerates the drying of Super Glue®.

Cyanoacrylite Solvent, acetone-based liquid that removes Super Glue®.

Draw, the degree of lift or play between the body of an electric guitar and the back of its tremolo.

Drift, settling or variance of a note shortly after it is struck.

Feedback, high-pitched microphonic frequencies produced by loose wires vibrating against each other.

Flat, 1. level on top. 2. lower than the ideal or desired pitch; opposite of sharp.

Fret, metal composite wire containing zinc, silver and nickel; shaped like a semicircle with a barbed stem.

Fretguard, plastic or cardboard guard shaped like a fretboard and placed between frets and strings to prevent the strings from damaging the frets during transport.

Fretwork, the forging, shaping and polishing of frets. Includes leveling, re-crowning, installing and burnishing.

Fretboard, slab of material, usually wood, that contains frets.

Fulcrum, pivot point or support on which a lever turns in raising or moving something. Bridge that can be rocked forward and backward with a lever.

Guitar Tuner, pitch or electronic reference device used to tune a guitar.

Hardtail, non-moving, non-fulcrum bridge.

Harmonic, generated tone whose rate of vibration is a precise multiple of that of a given fundamental tone.

Headstock, end of a neck containing the tuning keys and nut where the strings terminate.

Hex Key, tool shaped like a hexagon used to adjust various components on a guitar.

Humidifier, a device or machine that replaces moisture in an object or room.

Humidity, the amount of moisture in the air.

Hygrometer, gauge used to measure humidity.

Inertia Block, metal block that secures the counter balancing springs found in most fulcrum or tremolo style bridges.

Intonation, in unison, two notes matching in harmonic and fundamental pitch.

Locking String Nut, metal string nut that locks the strings into place.

Luthier, one who builds and repairs stringed instruments.

Luthiers Guild, a group of luthiers that meets for the betterment of their craft.

Magnifying Lamp, lamp containing a magnifying lens.

Maintenance, care, upkeep and support.

Micrometer, an instrument for measuring very small distances extremely accurately.

Miniature Needle File, single cut, carbide miniature file used for various repair projects on a guitar.

Neck Angle, the degree of angle the neck has in relationship to the bridge and top of a guitar.

Nut File, carbide, double-edged files available in various widths for cutting string slots into a nut.

Partial Re-fret, replacing some, but not all of the frets.

Pickup Balancing, equalizing the volume of a pickup in relationship to the strings and other pickups.

Precision Scale, 6" metal ruler used to measure in very small increments.

Radius, the circular area or distance limited by the sweep of such line. The circular arch of a fretboard, bridge saddle or string nut.

Re-Fret, total replacement of frets.

Relief, the degree of forebow or backbow in a neck.

Rule of 18, equation that determines string nut and fret placement. Scale/17.817 = distance from the nut to the first fret.

Set-in Neck, glued in or not a bolt on neck.

Sharp, above the desired pitch, opposite of flat.

Signal, electrical impulse.

Single Coil, pickup with only one coil.

Soldering Iron, electric iron that produced heat to melt solder.

Spring Claw, metal plate with hooks to hold tremolo springs to the inertia block.

Straight Edge, metal flat stock milled extremely flat used to gauge the forebow or backbow in a neck.

String Angle, the angle of a string in relationship to its beginning and termination.

String Ferrells, metal tubular inserts that hold the ball end of a string in place on an electric guitar.

String Nut, bridge-like, slotted object that holds the strings in place at the head-stock.

String Slots, channels cut at various depths and widths in the string nut.

String Spacing, the distance between each string slot.

String Tree, a disc, bar or T–shaped object that increases the angle of the string at the headstock.

String Winder, a device used to rapidly spin a tuning key button in order to speed up the process of re-stringing a guitar.

Tailpiece, apparatus that secures the strings of a guitar between the bridge and the tail block.

Temperament, varying degrees of tuning each string of an instrument to produce a more pleasant sound when multiple strings are played at the same time.

Transmit, force of movement, convey a signal.

Tremolo Springs, counter-balancing springs that keep a tremolo bridge level.

Tremolo System, bridge system that works on a fulcrum or pivot points.

Trussrod, metal rod inside the neck of a guitar used to stabilize it.

Trussrod Nut, used to adjust the relief in a neck.

Tunematic®, fixed bridge with individual saddles and thumbwheels.

Tuning Key, mechanical device used to tighten or loosen guitar strings.

Variable, something that is likely to change.

Velocity, swiftness or speed of motion.

Wire Cutters, cutting pliers used to cut wire.

Wood Glue, water-based resin.

X-Acto® Knife, small, sharp knife with a pencil-like handle.